P9-CDW-234

DATE DUE			

WEST CHESTER PUBLIC LIBRARY
415 NORTH CHURCH STREET AT LAFAYETTE
WEST CHESTER, PA 19380
610-696-1721

Mon. - Thurs.   9:30 a.m. - 8 p.m.
Fri. - Sat.   9:30 a.m. - 5 p.m.
Sunday   1:00 p.m. - 5 p.m.

QUARTER HORSES

by Victor Gentle and Janet Perry

Gareth Stevens Publishing
MILWAUKEE

For a free color catalog describing Gareth Stevens' list of high-quality books and multimedia programs, call 1-800-542-2595 (USA) or 1-800-461-9120 (Canada). Gareth Stevens Publishing's Fax: (414) 225-0377. See our catalog, too, on the World Wide Web: gsinc.com

Library of Congress Cataloging-in-Publication Data

Gentle, Victor.
    Quarter horses / by Victor Gentle and Janet Perry.
        p. cm. — (Great American horses: an imagination library series)
    Includes bibliographical references (p. 23) and index.
    Summary: Describes the physical features and other characteristics that have made the quarter horse one of the most popular breeds in America.
    ISBN 0-8368-2134-3 (lib. bdg.)
    1. Quarter horse—Juvenile literature. [1. Quarter horse. 2. Horses.]
I. Perry, Janet, 1960- . II. Title. III. Series: Gentle, Victor. Great American horses.
SF293.Q3G45   1998
636.1'33—dc21   98-14794

First published in 1998 by
Gareth Stevens Publishing
1555 North RiverCenter Drive, Suite 201
Milwaukee, WI 53212 USA

Text: Victor Gentle and Janet Perry
Page layout: Victor Gentle, Janet Perry, and Renee M. Bach
Cover design: Renee M. Bach
Series editor: Patricia Lantier-Sampon
Editorial assistants: Mary Dykstra and Diane Laska

Photo credits: Cover, pp. 5, 7, 9, 15, 17, 19, 21, & 22 © Bob Langrish; pp. 11 & 13 © The Kobal Collection

This edition © 1998 by Gareth Stevens, Inc. All rights reserved to Gareth Stevens, Inc. No part of this book may be reproduced, stored in a retrieval system, or transmitted in any form or by any means, electronic, mechanical, photocopying, recording, or otherwise without the prior written permission of the publisher except for the inclusion of brief quotations in an acknowledged review.

Printed in the United States of America

1 2 3 4 5 6 7 8 9 02 01 00 99 98

Front cover: Quarter Horses are strong, sturdy, handsome, and energetic — perfect horses for riding the range in great style!

TABLE OF CONTENTS

Words that appear in the glossary are printed in **boldface**
type the first time they occur in the text.

THE FIRST QUARTER HORSE

Experts say the first Quarter Horse was the baby of a Thoroughbred stallion (a male horse) and a Chickasaw Pony mare (a female horse).

A **breed** is a group of horses that all have the same physical features because people select and **breed** them for those features. A stallion and a mare **mate** and give birth to foals (baby horses) with the same features.

Thoroughbreds were brought to the American colonies from England. Quarter Horses' speed may come from them. Chickasaw Indians **bred** the Mustangs left by Spaniards along North America's southeastern coast to make Chickasaw Ponies. Quarter Horses' power may come from them.

Quarter Horses have solid-colored coats. They may be black, dark brown, chestnut, or **palomino**.

BUILT TO DO IT ALL

Whatever breeds their ancestors were, Quarter Horses are built to do it all.

All Quarter Horses have almost the same **conformation**, which allows them to handle all kinds of work. Quarter Horses are about fifteen **hands** high (5 feet, or 1.5 meters) at the **withers** and weigh from 1,000 to 1,100 pounds (450 to 500 kilograms).

By comparison, a Thoroughbred horse is about sixteen hands high and weighs about 1,200 pounds (545 kg).

There's a lot of strength in that tough, sturdy Quarter Horse body!

To warm up its legs before a race, this Quarter Horse trots around the track.

RUGGED GOOD LOOKS

Quarter Horses do not look very heavy, but they do have well-developed hip and thigh muscles. These muscles give the Quarter Horse the strength to burst into a full gallop from a standing start, or to stop cold in its tracks.

Quarter Horses look good in spite of their rugged lives. Their friendly eyes are large enough to catch even tiny movements. Their short, square noses are wide, so they can gulp air into their lungs for fast and furious work. Their round cheeks cover powerful jaws and strong teeth that chew through the toughest grasses. Quarter Horses get energy from food that other range animals cannot eat.

Quarter Horses often have white face and leg markings. The dark brown horse has a white blaze on its face and four white socks. Do others have similar markings?

STAR-QUALITY QUARTER HORSE

Although Quarter Horses were first bred in the southeastern United States, they are loved from coast to coast. They are best known as horse partners to cowboys in the West. Plus, they have those striking Hollywood good looks. So, of course, Quarter Horses starred in movies.

The famous movie and television cowboy, Roy Rogers, had a horse named Trigger. Trigger was half Quarter Horse and half Saddlebred, with palomino coloring. Roy and Trigger made movies between 1940 and 1960. People liked these movies because Roy Rogers could sing well and was handsome. They also loved Trigger because he did tricks and was at least as handsome as Roy.

Roy Rogers did not fool himself that he was a bigger star than Trigger. "Just as many fans are interested in seeing Trigger as they are in seeing me," Roy would say of his pal.

PARTY ANIMAL

Once, Trigger was invited to a big party in the ballroom of the elegant Astor Hotel in New York City. There, the beautiful horse danced, reared and pawed the air, played dead, and unknotted ropes with his mouth.

In movies, Trigger helped Roy get the job done. He trapped outlaws and pulled Roy from the jaws of death. The two stars were together in 87 movies and 101 television shows. Trigger even won two special awards — the Craven Award and the Patsy Award — for being "The Smartest Horse in the Movies."

Look at Trigger's large eyes. Horses' eyes catch all the action in almost a full circle because the pupils are on the sides of the head.

FAST FRIENDS

Quarter Horses are fast. They have been racing and winning for over two hundred years. No other horse has beaten a Quarter Horse in a quarter-mile race. What a record! In fact, that is why they are called "Quarter Horses."

Quarter Horses are a cowboy's best partner because they are almost fearless. As **cutting horses**, they have the courage to run into a herd of scared cattle and pull out a calf for branding and medication. They are so well trained that many cowboys will swear their horses do all of the thinking.

Home on the range. A cowboy, a Quarter Horse, a dog, and some cattle. Who's in charge here?

BUILDING BETTER HORSES

Quarter Horses are fine show horses. In Western riding competitions, they barrel-race, bulldog (which is similar to cutting), and go through their paces in Western and English Pleasure Riding classes. Quarter Horses are also used as polo ponies and in jumping events.

Quarter Horses are often bred with other horse breeds to improve the conformation of those breeds. Perhaps a little Mustang and Quarter Horse mare named Nita made history because she combined the best features of both breeds.

Waiting for the judges' decision, this Quarter Horse lets the world admire its fine looks. It doesn't look very fast now, but watch out!

"A SLEEPY LITTLE CRITTER THAT UNWINDS LIKE LIGHTNING!"

Nita and Steel Dust were two horses that helped make Quarter Horses famous. Nita was the horse that raced a train and won. Steel Dust was a **foundation sire**, or one of the founding fathers of the Quarter Horse breed.

In 1830, Nita raced the *Tom Thumb*, an experimental steam engine. She pulled a railway car faster than the *Tom Thumb*. The *Tom Thumb*'s engineers, however, said it was because their engine broke.

But Nita did not break. She was "the little *horse* that could."

A Quarter Horse is power in motion. This black beauty is **cantering**, a way of moving in a rocking and rhythmic three-beat gait.

"SOMEBODY WAKE THAT HORSE UP!"

The Texans jeered at Steel Dust, the stocky twelve-year-old plow horse from Illinois, brought in to run in a race. He looked slow and scruffy in the Texas heat. Like a sleepyhead, Steel Dust squinted at the bright sun from his half-blind eyes.

The Texans thought their sleek horse, Monmouth, could not lose the race, but Steel Dust burst forward from the start. By the end of the race, he was three entire horse lengths ahead of Monmouth. The Texans lost a lot of money, *and* they bought all of Steel Dust's foals.

For good looks, power, speed, and smarts, the Quarter Horse is the most popular breed of horse in America. The "sleepy little critter" does it all.

They're off! Jockeys hunch over to keep their weight off the rear muscles of the horse — that's the engine! Which Quarter Horse do you think will win?

DIAGRAM AND SCALE OF A HORSE

Here's how to measure a horse with a show of hands.
This beautiful Quarter Horse has ideal conformation.

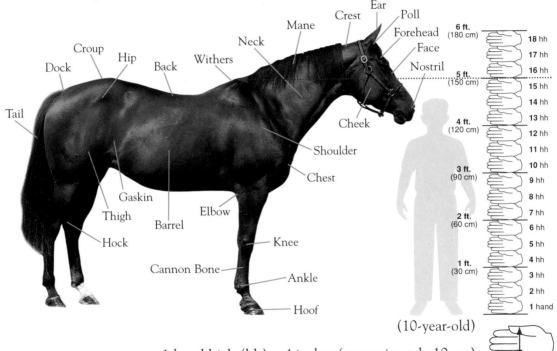

(10-year-old)

1 hand high (hh) = 4 inches (approximately 10 cm)

WHERE TO WRITE OR CALL FOR MORE INFORMATION

American Quarter Horse Association
P.O. Box 200
Amarillo, TX   79168
Phone: (806) 376-4811, Youth Extension: 282

MORE TO READ AND VIEW

Books (Nonfiction):   *The Complete Guides to Horses and Ponies* (series). Jackie Budd
    (Gareth Stevens)
A Day in the Life of a Horse Trainer. Charlotte McGuinn Freeman
    (Troll Associates)
Great American Horses (series). Victor Gentle and Janet Perry
    (Gareth Stevens)
Magnificent Horses of the World (series). Tomáš Míček and
    Dr. Hans-Jörg Schrenk (Gareth Stevens)
Wild Horse Magic for Kids. Animal Magic (series). Mark Henckel
    (Gareth Stevens)
Wild Horses of the Red Desert. Glen Rounds (Holiday House)

Books (Fiction):   *Black Gold.* Marguerite Henry (Rand, McNally)
Herds of Thunder, Manes of Gold. Edited by B. Coville (Doubleday)
Saddle Club (series). Bonnie Bryant. (Gareth Stevens)
Uncle Daney's Way. Jessie Haas. (Greenwillow)

Videos (Fiction):   *The Big Country.* (MGM Home Video)
National Velvet. (MGM/UA Home Video)

WEB SITES

American Quarter Horse Association:
www.aqha.com/aqhya.htm

For interactive games:
www.haynet.net/kidstuff.html

For general horse information:
www.haynet.net
www.bcm.nt
okstate.edu/breeds/horses

Due to the dynamic nature of the Internet, some web sites stay current longer than others. To find additional web sites, use a reliable search engine with one or more of the following keywords to help you locate information about horses: *Chickasaws, equitation, Mustangs, ranch, Saddlebreds,* and *Thoroughbreds.*

GLOSSARY

You can find these words on the pages listed. Reading a word in a sentence helps you understand it even better.

breed (n) — a group of horses that share the same features as a result of the careful selection of stallions and mares to produce foals 4, 6, 16, 20

breed (v), **bred** — to choose a stallion and a mare with certain features to produce foals with similar features 4, 10, 16, 18

cantering — moving in a rhythmic and rocking three-beat gait 18

conformation (KON-for-MAY-shun) — how a horse's body is built 6, 16, 22

cutting horse — a horse trained to separate a cow from the rest of a herd 14, 16

foundation sire — a male horse used to breed with mares to produce foals of a particular breed 18

hand — a unit used to measure horses that is equal to 4 inches (10.2 cm), about the width of the human hand 6, 22

mate (MAIT) — to breed a male and a female to produce young 4

palomino (PAL-oh-MEE-noh) — a color of horse that varies from pale cream to gold, with a light or white mane and tail 4, 10

withers (WITH-erz) — the ridge between the shoulder bones of a horse 6, 22

INDEX